Copyright 2020 - by Beth Costanzo

Visiting a real-life farm is one of the coolest things that you can do. Whether you are visiting a relative's farm or are visiting on a field trip there are lots of things to see and do. Farms usually have lots of animals to see. In the spring many baby animals born. These are some of the cutest creatures on the planet.

Here is a list of the **10 cutest baby animals** that will melt your heart. In fact, these are some of the cutest baby animals I have ever seen on the planet!

Let's begin!

www.adventuresofscubajack.com

NUMBER 10

www.adventuresofscubajack.com

Quack, Quack!

To start, we want to talk about ***baby ducks***. They are technically called ducklings. After baby ducks are born, they are led by their mothers half a mile (or more) to find an appropriate place for feeding and swimming. This is an extremely far walk for a baby duckling!

After the baby duckling is dry after hatching, it can start swimming. This is why you may see a mother duck swimming with a trail of baby ducklings behind her. However, they still cannot swim very well. They may struggle to keep up with their mother and siblings.

When they are born, baby ducks do not have feathers. They have a fuzz-like covering which makes them so photogenic. After they get older, they develop feathers and lose that fuzzy look. Because of this, try to see these baby ducks right after they are born. You're sure to get a great picture!

NUMBER 9

Oink, Oink!

Next, there are ***baby piglets***. Baby piglets are little pigs. When they are born, they have a pink color. They also have lighter skin compared to their mothers. As they age, their skin color tends to get darker and more like their parents.

Mothers give birth to baby piglets about twice per year. They often give birth to 12 piglets at one time. Baby pigs are known for their curiosity. They love sniffing around and exploring their environment. They aren't afraid to get dirty and love playing in the mud. Finally, one of the most interesting things about baby piglets is that they can have their own baby piglets very early. In fact, they can do it when they are six months old!

NUMBER 8

Baa, Baa!

From baby piglets, there are **baby lambs**. Both baby and adult lambs are known for their famous white fleece. When baby lambs are born, they weigh about five to eight pounds. These baby lambs are also born with tails, but they lose their tails as they get older.

After the baby lamb is born, it is fed and cared for by its mother. It takes about two or three months for baby lambs to consume food other than its mother's milk. In sum, baby lambs are extremely cute and photogenic. Be on the lookout for them when visiting your local firm.

NUMBER 7

Peep, peep!

Next, there are *baby chicks*. I'm sure you've seen baby chicks before. They are little chickens that have a bright yellow color. Baby chicks are born after their mother sits on their eggs for three weeks. When they hatch, baby chicks are wet and covered in the remnants from their egg. It starts taking on its bright yellow color when it dries itself off.

Baby chicks are born without teeth. While this may seem like a problem, they learn to eat by experimenting.

NUMBER 6

Baa, Baa!

Now, let's talk about *baby pygmy goats*. These animals are adorable. They have their famous black and white color that they later have as adults. Baby pygmy goats typically feed on many different foods, including corn, grains, and grasses. In the earliest days, they feed on milk.

Baby pygmy goats love to play. They are extremely active, whether they are playing by themselves or members of their family. You may be lucky to see them playing when you visit your local farm.

NUMBER 5

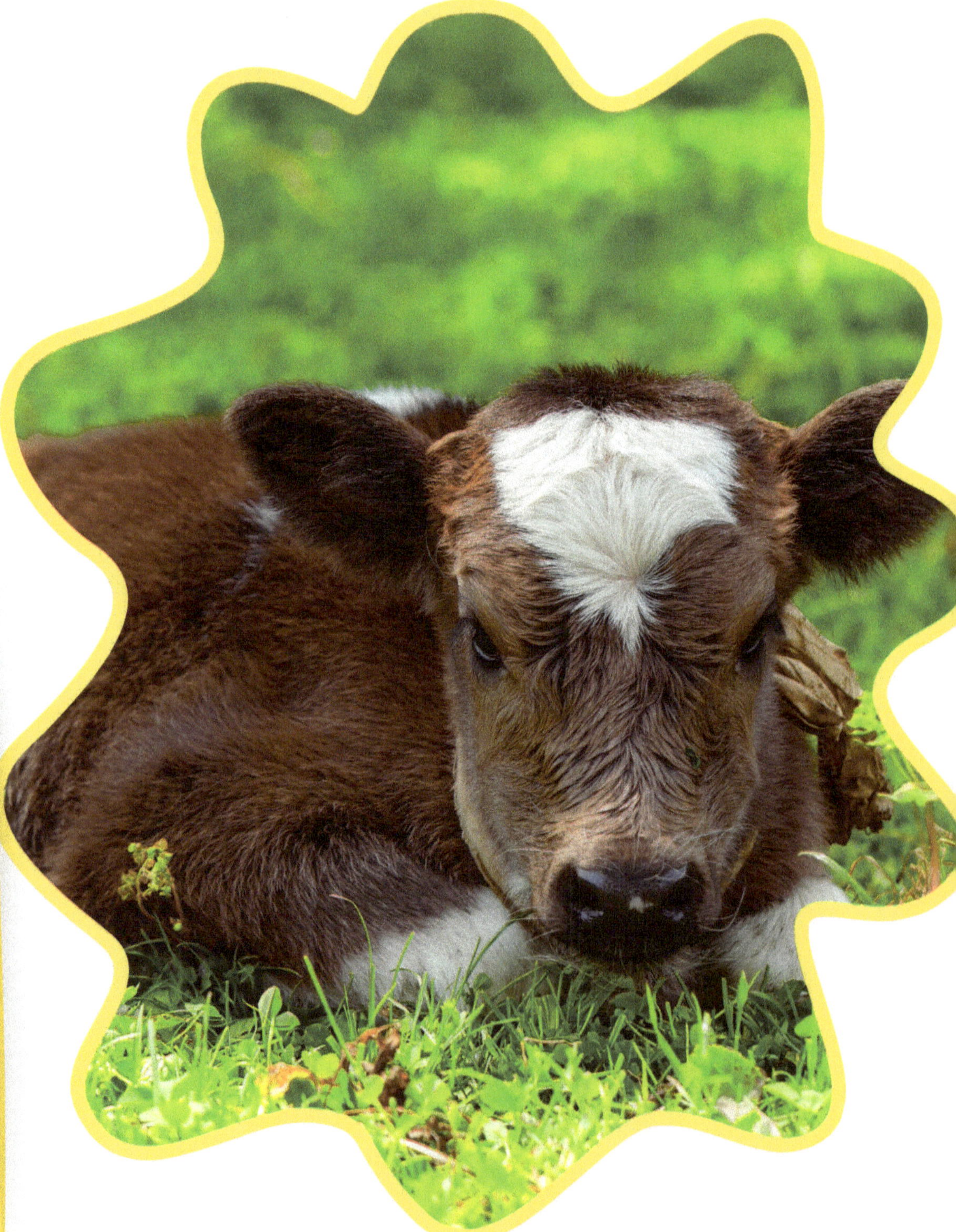

www.adventuresofscubajack.com

Moo, Moo!

Baby cows (called calves) are very heavy when they are born. In fact, they weigh around 60 to 100 pounds. That's a heavy baby! Even more impressive is that one hour after they are born, baby cows can stand, walk, and even nurse. Having said this, baby cows need to stay by their mothers for at least two days. They need to do so to get the milk they need to survive.

One of the coolest facts about baby cows is that their friends and family celebrate when they are born. The grownup cows gather around the baby cows to keep them safe and warm.

NUMBER 4

www.adventuresofscubajack.com

Neigh, Neigh!

Finally, ***baby foals*** are very cute. The foal is the actual name for a baby horse. Many foals are born at night and away from danger. Often, mothers give birth to a single foal, but twins are possible.

When baby foals are born, their legs are basically the same length as they will be when they're fully grown. However, it takes about one or two months for a baby foal to stand up and walk. They will feed on their mother's milk for several months.

NUMBER 3

www.adventuresofscubajack.com

Hee-haw!

This ***baby donkey*** is probably one of the cutest things you'll ever see.

Baby donkeys are called foals or a colt. Foals weigh between 19-30 pounds at birth and can stand 30 minutes after they are born.

The donkey is a member of the horse family. A female donkey is called a jenny or jennet. A male donkey is called a jack. Donkeys have a reputation for being stubborn. They are more cautious than horses. If a situation seems unsafe, they dig in their heels and won't move.

NUMBER 2

Meow, Meow!

This little face will melt your heart!
Kittens are totally dependent on their mother for survival. All Kittens are born with blue eyes. At birth kittens eyes are shut and they do not open until after seven to ten days.

After about two weeks, kittens quickly develop and begin to explore the world around them. A kitten's sense of hearing and smell is one of the best on the planet.

NUMBER 1

WE SAVED THE BEST LAST!
DRUM ROLL PLEASE...

**IT'S THE BABY BUNNY!
OMG!!! ADORABLE!**

NUMBER 1

www.adventuresofscubajack.com

Baby rabbits are called kits. When baby bunnies are first born they are small in size and they do not have hair and their eyes are closed. They drink milk from their mother bunny.

After a couple weeks their fur has come in and their eyes have opened. Around the 3rd week, you will see the babies getting more active and hopping around.

HERE ARE SOME FUN FARM ACTIVITIES TO DO AT HOME!

www.adventuresofscubajack.com

TRACING

Trace the letters below

F F F F F F F

f f f f f f f

B B B B B B B

b b b b b b b

TRACING

Trace the Phrase below then rewrite it

Baby Farm
Animals

COUNTING

Count the chicks and circle the correct answer

| 5 4 6 | 9 7 8 |
| 10 11 12 | 15 13 14 |

MATCHING

Match each baby animal with its parent

MAZE

Help the baby duck to find his mom

COLORING

CRAFT

Little Bunny

Let's make a cute Bunny together!

You will need:

Scissors
Glue
Coloring Pencils

Directions:

1- Cut the bunny parts
2- Glue back eyes and nose on the bunny's head
3- Glue the back and front paw to the bunny's body
4- Glue the bunny's head to the body
5- Glue the bunny's tail to the body
6- Color your cute Bunny!

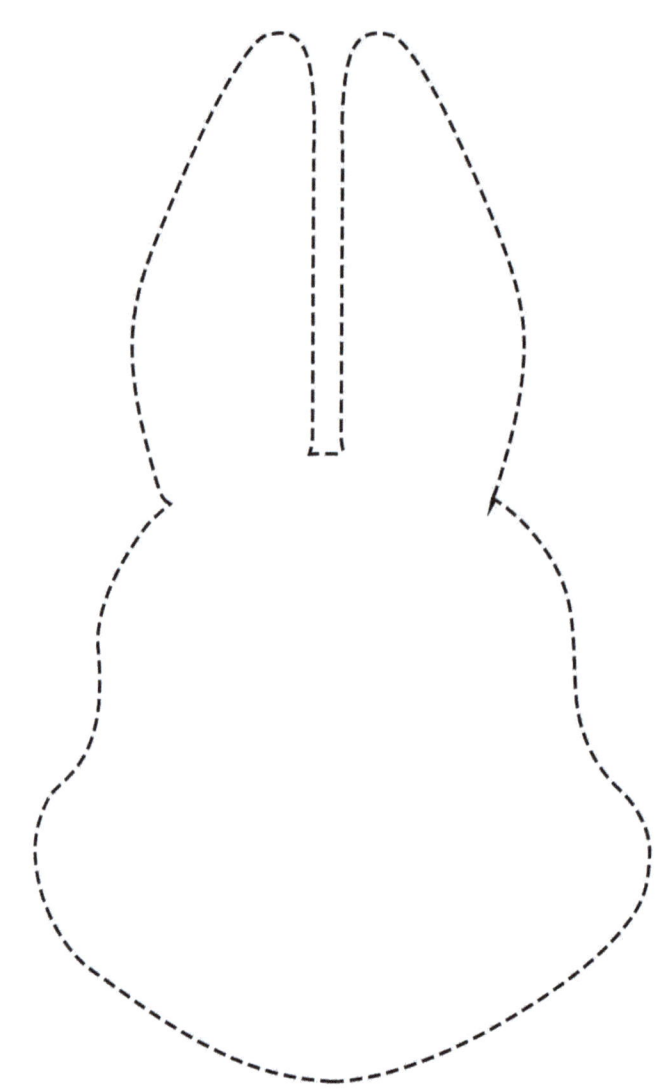
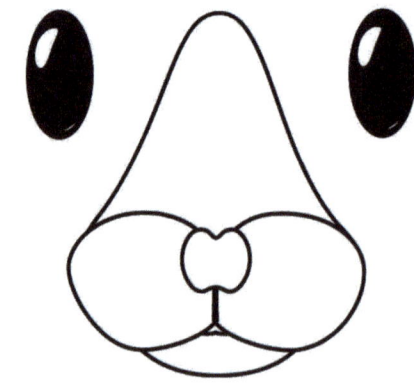

VISIT US AT
WWW.ADVENTURESOFSCUBAJACK.COM